My Cup Runneth Over

RAMON BENNETT

SHEKINAH

JERUSALEM

Copyright © 2016 Ramon Bennett
All Rights Reserved
First printed September 2016

ISBN 978-1-943423-19-4

Published in the United States by Shekinah Books LLC

Distributed in Israel by: Ramon Bennett,
P. O. Box 37111, Jerusalem 91370.
eMail: armofsalvation@mac.com.

SHEKINAH

Shekinah Books LLC
A division of *Arm of Salvation Ministries,* Jerusalem.

This paperback is subject to discounts for orders of 10 or more copies when purchased through Shekinah Books LLC. *My Cup Runneth Over* is also available as a Kindle e-Book or in PDF form. Further information can be obtained, and purchases of multiple hard copies or single PDF purchases may be made, by logging onto: *http://www.shekinahbooks.com.* All listed titles are available for purchase on *Amazon.com*

You prepare a table before me
*   in the presence of my enemies;*
you anoint my head with oil;
    my cup overflows (Psalms 23:5).

Thou preparest a table before me
*   in the presence of mine enemies:*
thou anointest my head with oil;
    my cup runneth over
                    (Psalms 23:5 KJV).

Contents

There is an heart-warming story in the gospel of Luke about two followers of Jesus who, on the third day following the crucifixion, were walking from Jerusalem to a little town named Emmaus. As they walked together they both spoke about and debated the events that had taken place, and they shared their hopes that were seemingly dashed with the death of Jesus.

As they walked and talked together, the resurrected Jesus joined them, but they were prevented from recognizing him. Jesus asked them what they were talking about and why they had such sad countenances. They told this apparent "stranger" about Jesus of Nazareth, a mighty prophet in word and deed, whom the chief priests and rulers had condemned to death and delivered up to the Romans, who had crucified Him. They told this "stranger" how they had hoped Jesus was the One who would redeem Israel, and they also told him about a "wild" tale told to them by some of the women followers about how they had gone to the tomb and had seen angels, who had told them Jesus was alive.

Jesus chided the two travelers for being slow to believe what the prophets had foretold about the Christ and his suffering, and then He walked them through all the Scriptures, from Moses and the Prophets, explaining everything concerning Himself.

The two disciples were turning into an inn for the night and Jesus made as if he would continue on, but they persuaded him to stay with them that night. As they sat down to eat, Jesus took bread, blessed it, and gave it to them and their eyes were opened and they recognized Him, then He vanished from their sight. They completely lost interest in staying at the inn for the night and began hurrying back to Jerusalem. They said to one another:

> **Did not our heart burn within us while He talked with us on the road, and while He opened the Scriptures to us?"**
>
> (Luke 24:32).

This little book is an attempt to set readers' hearts burning, like the burning hearts of the two disciples as Jesus opened to them spiritual truths concerning Himself.

My Cup

I want to tell readers another story, it is also a true story. My story is centered around a cup that I purchased in a small village in the middle of China in 1989, for a princely sum equivalent to one U.S. Dollar. It is a particularly handsome cup, larger even than most coffee mugs, and it has a lid to keep hot contents hot for longer periods. On the outside of the cup there is a coating of black porcelain, which in turn is covered with a multitude of small, hand-painted, multicolored flowers (picture on the cover). The cup had a rather thin handle for its size and I wondered if it would not break with regular use.

I bought the cup because it was big and had caught my eye while browsing among stalls in an open-air market. My wife and I were the only foreigners in a bustling sea of ethnic Chinese peasants selling their wares. The cup was a splendid example of Chinese handcraft and I wanted it as a souvenir, but as a practical item that could be used and not just another piece of tourist bric-a-brac that is relegated to a shelf, forgotten, and which gathers its own weight in dust.

I carried the cup around for the rest of that extensive speaking tour for a full six months before I arrived home again, happily with the cup in one piece, and finally able to use it. The cup quickly became my favorite, it soon became the exclusive cup from which I drank hot beverages at home.

I have a small office at roof level, one floor above our apartment in downtown Jerusalem. Each morning I would take a cup of coffee or tea up twenty stone steps to my office, and then bring it down again at lunchtime, rinse and refill it, before taking it back to my office until I deemed my workday over, at which time I would bring the cup down again and wash it once more. This routine remained the same for the years I was at home and not traveling. However, one day in June 1996, as I was going up to my office with coffee in my beloved cup, the toe of my sandal caught on a step and I tripped and fell. I tried to protect the cup as I fell, badly skinning and bruising both of my arms, but the cup still banged down onto the stone steps, splashing coffee about. There was then a very bad crack at the back of the cup, close to the handle, from the top almost to its base. Part of the black ceramic finish had chipped off around the crack, as had some of the brightly colored flowers. When I came down at the end of the day my wife Zipporah attempted to console me by saying, "It could last for years like that," but I was saddened.

I was grateful that the cup did not actually leak, but over the coming weeks and months the crack became increasingly discolored from coffee and tea and, as the crack was around the back of the cup, it appeared to mock me at my every sip. However, one day as I was rinsing the cup, it seemed as if the crack was no longer there. I immediately dismissed the notion because I "knew" that such a thing could not be. It was only later that I purposely inspected the cup, feeling a little foolish for doing so, but the crack was indeed no longer visible. I turned the cup around looking at it carefully and then got a magnifying glass, but there was no crack and not sign of there ever having been a crack.

The black ceramic finish was now perfect, as were all the flowers and glazing. I called my wife, Zipporah, into the kitchen, showed her the cup and exclaimed, "God has healed my cup!" Zipporah took the cup, turned it around and around, then said, "How did He do that!?"

The "healing" of the cup shows the extraordinary love God has for His children. At no time did I ever lament the damaging of the cup to God, and it would never have entered my mind to ask Him to "fix" it. But He knew that I was saddened by the dreadful crack in my beloved cup and decided, on His own volition, to fix it, and for no other reason than that He loved me and wanted to make that truth acutely clear. We can no more doubt God's love than we can question our own existence. God not only does what we ask of Him, but He also does what we do not ask of Him—that is the wonder of God's nature. We cannot "prove" the existence of God, but the episode of my cup being made whole again after it had been so badly cracked and damaged "proves" there is a far higher power at work among those who **believe**.

That 1996 incident with the cup has had an eternal impact on my life. Twenty years later that miraculous touch of love continues to impact Zipporah and me, and to whomever we tell the story. Who has ever before heard of a cracked and damaged cup being supernaturally made new again? But did God not say: *"I will do **marvels** such as have not been done in all the earth"*? (Exodus 34:10).

With God, both the actual and the possible are subject to His command and control—everything is obedient to the voice of God, **even cups!** And what Jesus said to the Jews two thousand years ago, he would say to us today:

> *Even though you do not believe Me,* **believe the works that I do**" (John 10:38).

Over the years a number of supernatural miracles have happened before my eyes, but most are now mere memories and recounting them to others provides no proof that the miracles actually took place—except in the case of my cracked cup that God healed on His own initiative. It is one thing to see a generator run for hours without gas (petrol) and another to be miraculously healed of a debilitating disease, but having an object that was badly cracked, chipped and stained suddenly being made whole and perfect again, is quite another matter. We still have that cup and each time it was used we would talk about when and how it was badly damaged. It is a constant reminder to us of God's love and wondrous power.

In October 2014 we finally put the cup out to pasture, that is, we put it on display in our china cabinet. We felt we would never forgive ourselves if we broke that cup after the Lord had made it new again; we wanted always to see it whole and continue remembering, *forever*. To experience a miracle like that—and the cup has been examined through a magnifying glass more than once—leaves me in no doubt that God, according to His word, will raise the dead *"on the last day"* (John 6:40, 6:44, 6:54) without a second thought. Our God is quite beyond comprehension—He is not restricted by boundaries, He is here, there, and everywhere—there is no place and can be no place where God is not.

Christian, Or Believer?

Leaving the story of the cup for a while, let me really start at the beginning. I am a believer in the Lord Jesus Christ, I am a follower of His. I could just as easily have said that I am a Christian, but there are multitudes who claim to be Christian, but who, in reality, speak and act not so very differently than do outright heathens, and these give Christians and the Church a bad name. Followers of Christ are **believers in Jesus, in His words, and in His God**—our heavenly Father. Believers in Jesus are to be found everywhere, in the thousands, in both Protestant and Catholic churches. Their skin colors come in many hues and they live all over the world. What sets believers in the Lord Jesus Christ apart from the average, run-of-the-mill Christian, is that they really do "*believe*." Saying this is not intended to suggest that believers in Jesus are somehow "superior" to other Christians, but it *is* meant to propose to you that there is a difference between being a "*Christian*" and being a "*believer*" in Jesus Christ and in the words that He spoke, many of which have been handed down to us in the gospels of Matthew, Mark, Luke and John. We would do well to ingest those words of Jesus, absorbing them until obeying them becomes second nature.

I became a Christian in 1965. Prior to that I was a godless, foul-mouthed, heavy-smoking, alcohol swilling pagan who suffered the most dreadful migraine headaches. In June 1965 I came to believe that Jesus was God's *only begotten Son*, and that He purposely died on a Roman cross on a hill in Jerusalem, to give all mankind the opportunity to turn— to repent—from their rebellion against God and receive fullness of life here on earth and eternal life in the hereafter.

Even though I believed that Jesus was God's *only begotten Son*, and through believing I had become a child of God (John 1:12) and had eternal life, I sensed there was something missing. My life had changed very much for the better. I enjoyed reading the Bible, going to church and having fellowship with other Christians, but there was a void, an emptiness in my soul. Something was missing.

Two years later, in August 1967, the void was still very evident to me. I was self-employed so determined to seek God with a whole heart and refused to begin my day's work until after I had spent premium time reading and meditating on the Bible, speaking to God in prayer, and listening for what He might have to say to me. One particular day I had completed my reading and, as was my habit, knelt down in front of my office desk and prayed. I told God again about my feeling about their being something akin to a void in my soul, that I felt something was missing. I told God that I wanted to go on with Him, that I wanted to serve Him; there was such a hunger in my soul for more of God.

After some time I finished praying that day and opened my eyes. I was still kneeling at my desk and my Bible remained open, just inches beneath my nose. A verse caught my attention, and in it Jesus said:

> *If you then, being evil, know how to give good gifts to your children: how much more shall your heavenly Father give the Holy Spirit to them that ask him?*
>
> (Luke 11:13).

I instinctively knew that it was the Lord placing this verse before me. I said softly, "Father, give me the Holy Spirit." And my life has never been the same since.

The Lord Is The God Of The Miraculous

It is difficult to describe a miracle, any miracle. That day, when I said, "Father, give me the Holy Spirit," something akin to a bucket of thick, warm liquid seemed to be pouring out on my head. The sensation of that liquid ran slowly down my body, down my arms, down my legs and over my feet. That experience, so many years ago, is as real and as vivid to me today as it was at the time. Half a century has passed since then, but the passing of time has not erased the memory or the sensation of that thick, warm liquid running all over me. I was a different person following that momentous morning. I felt different, and my faith level leapt upwards. I had believed that Jesus was God's *only begotten Son* and that He died on that cross for all mankind, and believing that had changed me for the better. Now I had taken Jesus at His word and had asked the Father for the Holy Spirit, and it was immediately poured out upon me. I was now at the earliest stage of becoming a "***believer***" in Jesus.

What I have just described above, so inadequately, but nevertheless described as best I can, dramatically changed my life. A few days after the life-changing event I was kneeling on my living room floor worshiping the Lord with my hands raised. For some months I had experienced an irregular pain in my left elbow, apparently from driving my car with the driver's window open. The pain would come each time there was no movement of the arm for a minute or two, but would immediately disappear when the arm was moved. On this particular day, my worshiping, with my hands raised, was constantly being interrupted because it was necessary for me to bring my arm down each few minutes. After dropping my arm down four or five times in order to relieve the distress, I cried out in frustration, "Oh, Lord, take it away!" Immediately the pain disappeared! It has never returned. This was my first personal experience of the healing power of Jesus and it propelled me forward in the pursuit of becoming more of a "*believer*" in Jesus, and in His words.

After being empowered by the Holy Spirit the Bible really came alive for me and I would read and devour it for hours every day. I would also pray up a storm in prayer meetings and whenever else the occasion permitted; I was soon to be thrust into street evangelism. And from that day to this I have never suffered a migraine headache.

However, many Christians do not "*believe*" that being "*clothed*," or "*empowered*," or "*filled*" with *the Holy Spirit* (Luke 24:49) is necessary; they do not "*believe*" that it is for today, which brings me back to the point that I made earlier: what sets a "*believer*" in the Lord Jesus Christ apart from the average, run-of-the-mill **Christian**, is that a "*believer*" really does "*believe*." They "*believe*" that miracles are for today, and because they "*believe*" that miracles are for today they experience them! Those that do not "*believe*," are nothing less than "*unbelievers*" in Jesus. Worse, they prevent miracles from happening:

> *He did not do many mighty works there because of their unbelief*
>
> (Matthew 13:58).

Many "*unbelievers*" in Jesus also express incredulity about the devil, about his very existence—they all the more readily become his prey.

God says, "*For I the Lord do not change*" (Malachi 3:6), and of Jesus it is written: "*Jesus Christ is the same yesterday, today, and forever*" (Hebrews 13:8). So, if God does not change, and Jesus, who was God incarnate, is *the same yesterday, today, and forever,* how is it that a large part of the Church hold to the belief that both God and Jesus must have changed because they hold that being "*clothed with power from on high*" (Luke 24:49) is no longer relevant, and that miracles are no longer for today?

Jesus had breathed on the disciples and said, *"Receive the Holy Spirit"* (John 20:22), and later He said:

Behold, I am sending the promise of my Father upon you. But stay in the city until you are clothed with power from on high (Luke 24:49).

All those coming to know Jesus in a personal way receive a measure to *the Holy Spirit*, but there is more to be had and those willing to wait with *expectation* for the *promise* of the *Father* will get *"clothed with power from on high."* A weightlifter cannot lift weights if he has insufficient muscle power. A Church that has no *Holy Spirit power* cannot change a baby's diapers let alone a sick and dying world.

I am talking about *the power of the Holy Spirit*, not the plethora of ridiculous "Pentecostal" extremisms like swinging from chandeliers or making people speak in "tongues." I am an advocate of good old-fashioned *Holy Spirit power* that changes people, the workplace, and the world. Little more than a handful of disciples in the Upper Room, *"clothed with power from on high,"* changed the known world. Since then, the expanding number of "**unbelievers**" both in Jesus and miracles have reduced a vibrant early Church into an impotent, ugly, 21st-century Church. Many churches and denominations today want nothing to do with *the Holy Spirit,* and miracles, as often as not, are put down to being works of the devil. And we wonder why, after almost two thousand years, Christianity is now becoming a minority religious movement under the patronage of Someone in whom it has no faith?

Also, in the minds of many Christian "**unbelievers**," both the Father and the Son must continually undergo change, because a great many churches now accept and participate in homosexual and same-sex marriages, and not a few have homosexual and lesbian ministers. These churches and their leaders openly condone what God steadfastly condemns:

> *If a man lies with a male as he lies with a woman, both of them have committed **an abomination*** (Leviticus 20:13).

> *women exchanged the natural use for what is against nature* (Romans 1:26).

Aeons ago, in a similar situation God Almighty said:

*They have **set their abominations** in the house that is called by my name"*
                                                    (Jeremiah 7:20).

And the Church today is where Jesus has put His name. Some denominations and branches of the Church are both an affront and an abomination to God and a day of reckoning is coming. Today's Church has largely become a derailed institution for "**unbelievers**" who continue in sin yet still try to move the train, even though it is off the rails, wrecked and engineless.

Those Who Believe In His Name

Jesus said to the father of the epileptic boy:

*If you can **believe**, all things are possible to him who **believes*** (Mark 9:23).

And when they told the ruler of the synagogue that his daughter was dead, Jesus overhead and said: *"Do not be afraid; only **believe**, and **she will be made well**"* (Luke 8:50).

The Christian life is all about believing. To even begin the Christian walk one has to start with **believing**:

*as many as received Him, to them He gave the right to become children of God, to those who **believe in His name***

(John 1:12).

Believing in the name of Jesus means believing in all that Jesus *is* and all that He **has said**. **Unbelief** is already **disobedience**. If we do not **believe** how can we reproduce our own kind? Jesus said:

*I do not pray for these alone, but also **for those who will believe in Me through their word***" (John 17:20).

Most Christians teeter on the brink of being a believer, they never share with those outside of the church what they half-heartedly believe. Jesus says: *"Let not your heart be troubled; you believe in God, **believe also in Me**"* (John 14:1). The brother of the Lord said: **"You believe that there is one God. You do well. Even the demons believe—and tremble!"** (James 2:19). To **believe** is to **act upon** that **belief**. How will your family, friends, neighbors and work colleagues know about salvation and eternal life unless you tell them?

*How then shall they call on Him in whom they **have not believed**? And **how shall*** *they believe in Him of whom they have not heard? And how shall they hear without a preacher?* (Romans 10:14).

We are duty bound to share the gospel and propagate God's good news to man. We fail to warn the lawless and morally wrong to the peril of our own souls:

When I say to the wicked, "You shall surely die," and you give him no warning, nor speak to warn the wicked from his wicked way, to save his life, that same wicked man shall die in his iniquity; but his blood I will require at your hand (Ezekiel 3:18).

Do I have any pleasure at all that the wicked should die?" says the Lord God, "and not that he should turn from his ways and live? (Ezekiel 18:23).

Once *"clothed with power from on high"* even the quietest "church mouse" becomes a powerhouse of the Holy Spirit and a very real threat to the forces of the devil. But of course, you must first *"believe"* that it is relevant for today—

Ask, and it will be given to you; seek, and you will find; knock, and it will be opened to you" (Matthew 7:7).

The Angel of God appeared to Gideon and said:

> *The Lord is with you, you mighty man of valor! Gideon said to Him, "O my lord, **if the Lord is with us ... where are all His miracles?**"* (Judges 6:12–13).

Wherever the presence of God is there are miracles, and my beloved cup is proof enough of that. **Expect** miracles, and you will **experience** miracles.

Faith = Belief

Next to Jesus, Abraham is the most oft-mentioned person in the Bible connected with faith. We should ask ourselves why Abraham plays such an important part in the Scriptures. Abraham lived a full life and, as is the manner of man, he became old. He also remained childless, without a natural heir. Abraham's wife, Sarai, later called Sarah, was barren from her youth and, as is the manner of the female of the species of man, progressed past beyond the age of childbearing. We now pick up Abraham's story in Chapter 15 of Genesis. Speaking to the Lord Abram said:

> *Lord God, what will You give me, seeing I go childless, and the heir of my house is*

Eliezer of Damascus? Then Abram said, "Look, You have given me no offspring; indeed one born in my house is my heir!"

*And behold, the word of the Lord came to him, saying, "This one shall not be your heir, but **one who will come from your own body shall be your heir.**" Then He brought him outside and said, "Look now toward heaven, and count the stars if you are able to number them." And He said to him, "So shall your descendants be." And **he believed the Lord**, and He counted it to him as righteousness* (Genesis 15:2–6).

Count Nikolaus von Zinzendorf (1700–1760) said: "***To believe against hope is the root of the gift of miracles.***" Abraham believed against hope; he believed God for the impossible and by so doing cemented his relationship with God Almighty: "***Abraham believed God***, *and it was counted to him as righteousness—**and he was called a friend of God**" (James 2:23). Abraham is the only person in the Bible to be called God's friend, and it was not just a one-off occurrence:

*But you, Israel, are My servant, Jacob whom I have chosen, **the descendants of Abraham My friend** (Isaiah 41:8).*

> *Are You not our God, who drove out the inhabitants of this land before your people Israel, and gave it to **the descendants of Abraham Your friend** forever?*
>
> (2Chronicles 20:7).

What set Abraham apart from all others was the simple fact that *"**he believed God**,"* and this greatly endeared Abraham to the *Lord of the universe* and the Lord called Abraham *"**My friend**."* Most Christians would say, in all sincerity, "I believe God," or "I believe Jesus." But is this fact, or is this fantasy? Judging by what we read in the books of the Old Testament, God had few friends.

In the New Testament we have Jesus, who was God incarnate, and He says to us:

> *You are My friends **if you do whatever I command you***" (John 15:14).

In order to be classified as a *"**friend**"* of Jesus we need to keep **all** of His commandments— **doing whatever He commands us**, not just doing what we feel like doing.

In the Old Testament God emphatically says, *"**I hate divorce**"* (Malachi 2:16), and in the New Testament Jesus emphatically says:

What God has joined together, let not man separate...I say to you: **whoever divorces his wife, except for sexual immorality, and marries another, commits adultery**

(Matthew 19:6, 9).

Going further, the Apostle Paul emphatically says: *"And a husband is not to divorce his wife"* (1Corinthians 7:11). Yet, with God the Father, God the Son, and the great Apostle Paul so emphatically against divorce, hundreds of thousands of "Christians" have divorced their spouses. Statistics even indicate that the divorce rate is actually higher within the Church than it is outside the Church among the agnostics and atheists. Obviously, such people within the Church are not **"friends"** of Jesus because they do not do what Jesus and His apostles commands. And so we return again to what was written earlier, that multitudes of professing Christians are, in reality, **unbelievers** in God, Jesus, and New Testament teaching, because they openly do what they are commanded not to do. God Almighty is *"the justifier of the one who* **has faith in Jesus**" (Romans 3:26). God is the justifier of all those who have *"faith in Jesus,"*

He is not the justifier of those who merely have some sort of faith **about** Jesus.

Asking In The Name Of Jesus

Jesus said: *"If you ask anything **in My name**, I will do it"* (John 14:14). But there are two provisos attached to this. The first being that what we ask for must align with the will of God:

> *Now this is the confidence that we have in Him, that if we ask **anything according to His will**, He hears us"* (1John 5:14).

An example of praying the will of God would be that the salvation of individuals and groups is dear to the heart of God; He is **"not willing that any should perish but that all should come to repentance"** (2Peter 3:9). Therefore, we are praying on solid ground whenever we pray for an individual or a group's salvation; but we must still **believe** for that salvation with **confidence** and an **expectation** of it coming to pass.

The second proviso is that we ask in His **name**. Now, asking **in the name of Jesus** does not mean tacking His name onto the end of a prayer, as in "…in Jesus' name, Amen." The **name** of Jesus means all that He is. Jesus was

God incarnate and shares the same name: "*I and My Father are one*" (John 10:30). And in the Book of Exodus God Almighty told Moses that He would pass before him and **proclaim His name**. And then we read:

> *Now the Lord descended in the cloud and stood with him there, and proclaimed **the name of the Lord**. And the Lord passed before him **and proclaimed**, "The Lord, the Lord God, **merciful** and **gracious**, longsuffering, and abounding in goodness and **truth**, keeping mercy for thousands, forgiving iniquity and transgression and sin, by no means clearing the guilty, visiting the iniquity of the fathers upon the children and the children's children to the third and the fourth generation"*
> (Exodus 34:5–7).

I only emphasized God Almighty's attributes of **mercy**, **grace**, and **truth** because we find those same attributes written of Jesus:

> *And the Word became flesh and dwelt among us, and we beheld His glory, the glory as of the only begotten of the Father, full of **grace** and **truth*** (John 1:14).

*For the law was given through Moses, but **grace** and **truth** came through Jesus Christ (John 1:17).*

*Jesus said to him, 'I am the way, the **truth**, and the life. No one comes to the Father except through Me (John 14:6).*

When we come to Jesus and truly believe *in* Him we receive a measure of the Holy Spirit, which is given as a guarantee of our heavenly inheritance through Jesus:

*In Him you also trusted, after you heard the word of **truth**, the gospel of your salvation; in whom also, having **believed**, you were sealed with the **Holy Spirit** of promise, who is the guarantee of our inheritance until the redemption of the purchased possession, to the praise of His glory (Ephesians 1:13).*

Being recipients of **the Holy Spirit** we should therefore exhibit its fruit:

the fruit of the Spirit is love, joy, peace, longsuffering, kindness, goodness, faithfulness, gentleness, self-control (Galatians 5:22);

all goodness, righteousness, and truth
(Ephesians 5:9).

The name of Jesus is an embodiment of all the fruits of the Spirit, thus our petitions to God our Father must first be in accordance with His will, and then rendered in the spirit of all that is *good*, *true*, and *holy*; then we can have the *confidence*, the *expectation*, that we shall receive all that we ask for.

Hearing And Listening

We begin our Christian walk as believers in Jesus, but we seem to go downhill from that point, because we begin consciously and unconsciously picking and choosing which parts of the Bible we will believe and which parts we will not. This is usually the fault of the Church. Congregations are force-fed what pastors personally believe, and people will always become what their leaders are. Christians can go off the rails by unwittingly following someone who has himself been derailed for years, whether he be a conservative, charismatic or pentecostal. None of these three persuasions are free from unbelief and error. The only person to follow is the Lord Jesus Christ, and this entails *fully* believing and **obeying** what He is known to have said.

When Jesus was on the Mount of Transfiguration with Peter, James, and John,

> *a bright cloud overshadowed them; and suddenly a voice came out of the cloud, saying, "This is My beloved Son, in whom I am well pleased.* **Hear Him!**"

(Matthew 17:5).

God Almighty spoke to the three disciples from heaven and His words were recorded for posterity: "*This is My beloved Son.* **Hear Him!**" When God says, "**Hear Him!**," and tells us to listen to His Son, He means for us to **hear**, to **believe**, and to **obey**. God Almighty enforces this message and adds His proviso: "*Incline your ear, and come to Me.* **Hear, and your soul shall live**" (Isaiah 55:3). Many churchgoers listen, but few actually hear. They are no different to those with whom God had lost patience with in yesteryear: "*I have spoken to you persistently, but* **you have not listened to me**" (Jeremiah 35:14). We need to listen, because there are sombre implications if we do not:

*Take heed **what you hear**. With the same measure you use, it will be measured to you; and **to you who hear, more will be given***" (Mark 4:24).

Believe!

The word "*believe*" is used eighty-three times throughout the gospels, only four times is the use not connected with faith. Jesus did not use the word "*believe*" so many times because He was short of a synonym. He used it often because it is imperative that we do **believe** what He said and then **act upon** what He said. If Jesus were to physically visit an average church on any given Sunday and say, "**all things are possible** *to him who* **believes**" (Mark 9:23), congregants may well say to themselves, "I don't **believe** that!" If He were to say "*If you have **faith as a mustard seed**, you will say to this **mountain**, 'Move from here to there,' and it will move; and **nothing will be impossible** for you* (Matthew 17:20), most of the congregation would likely say something akin to: "Nonsense! Don't be ridiculous!" This is because we have become what Jesus repeatedly labeled his disciples as: "*O you of **little faith***" (Matthew 8:26). Jesus was not advocating that we physically move mountains, He was saying that with real *faith* nothing is impossible. Simply put, *faith* is **unutterable trust** in God.

When we worry about everyday things we prove we have fallen into the same category of those whom Jesus reprimanded with His, "*O you of little faith.*"

> *So why do you **worry** about clothing? Consider the lilies of the field, how they grow: they neither toil nor spin; and yet I say to you that even Solomon in all his glory was not arrayed like one of these. Now if God so clothes the grass of the field, which today is, and tomorrow is thrown into the oven, **will He not much more clothe you, O you of little faith**? Therefore do not **worry**, saying, "What shall we **eat**?" or "What shall we **drink**?" or "What shall we **wear**?" For after all these things the nations seek. For your heavenly Father **knows** that **you need** all these things* (Matthew 6:28–32).

Probably, we have all **read** the above homily in Matthew's gospel dozens of times, but do we really **believe** what Jesus said? Now, "*God is* *love*" (1John 4:16) and it is written—"***No good thing will He withhold*** *from those who walk uprightly*" (Psalms 84:11). Arguably, the best known Psalm is Psalm 23, which begins: "*The Lord is my shepherd,* ***I shall not want.***" Do we ***believe*** that? Jesus is the *Good Shepherd* and that a shepherd watches over and tends his flock, ensuring the sheep have everything they need in the way of food and drink.

Worrying is a sin. God will meet our every ***need*** (***not*** our every ***want***) ***if*** we ***believe***. Using Credit Cards to run up debt is merely giving it to ***lust*** for things we cannot afford and this is "***covetousness, which is idolatry***" (Colossians 3:5). Saying, "I can't," is little short of rebellion and should be replaced by, "***I can do all things*** *through Christ who strengthens me*" (Philippians 4:13).

What we know as "The Lord's Prayer" guides our line of praying. We should indeed ask God for our necessary bread and then accept that it will be so, because it is God's will that we are fed and watered, but never take for granted what is placed on our tables, ensure that God is properly thanked for everything and given credit for His goodness from a grateful heart.

An illustration of gratitude and ingratitude happened one particular day in the region of Galilee. Jesus was met by ten lepers who cried out to Him from a distance for mercy. In response, He told them to go and show themselves to the priests, and as they went they became clean. One of the men, a Samaritan, when he saw that he was healed returned, loudly praising God, and kneeling at the feet of Jesus he gave Him thanks. Jesus said,

> *Were there not ten cleansed? But where are the nine? Were there not any found who returned to give glory to God except this foreigner?" And He said to him, "Arise, go your way. Your faith has made you well"* (Luke 17:17–19).

Jesus was offended by the very fact that only one out of the ten men cleansed was grateful to God—*there is nothing so ugly and hurtful as ingratitude*. Ingratitude will quickly block the channel through which God's blessings flow. Not even God Almighty likes ungrateful children.

What Is faith?

Faith is the same as sitting down upon a chair. We take it for granted that a chair is meant for sitting on. We do not deliberate about whether a chair will hold our weight; we just pull one up and sit down, convinced from childhood that chairs are for sitting on and we have natural faith for that: "*Now faith is the* **assurance** *of things* **hoped** *for, the* **conviction** *of things not seen*" (Hebrews 11:1).

Let me rephrase that: **faith** *is the* **assurance** *of things* **expected**, *the* **conviction** *of things not seen*. It is chair-type faith. Now, biblical "**hope**" is not the political "hope-so" variety. Biblical **hope** is an **expectation** of receiving that which is not yet seen in the actual, as in: "*Then God said, 'Let there be light'; and there was light*" (Genesis 1:3). That is true biblical "**hope**," the **expectation**, the **conviction** of things not seen. There had never, ever been light until God Almighty called it forth out of darkness on the first day of creation. The Sun and the Moon were not made until the fourth day of creation.

We need to live in the same state of **expectation**, being absolutely **convinced** that Jesus is God, that His word is **truth**, and that

God's Spirit dwells **in us**—*"If the Spirit of Him who raised Jesus from the dead dwells in you, He who raised Christ from the dead will also give life to your mortal bodies through His Spirit who **dwells in you*** (Romans 8:11). We need to **believe** more and move out of the natural into the **supernatural realm where God lives**: **"God, who gives life to the dead and calls those things which do not exist as though they did"** (Romans 4:17). It is a matter of *faith*, and *faith* is **believing against hope**.

Be It According To Your Faith

One day, as Jesus was leaving Jericho, a blind beggar named Bartimaeus heard that He was passing by and repeatedly cried out with a loud voice, *"Jesus, Son of David, have mercy on me!"* (Mark 10:47–48). Jesus heard the man's cry and called for Bartimaeus to come to Him.

Throwing aside his cloak, he got up and came to Jesus (Mark 10:50). *So Jesus said to him,* **"What do you want Me to do for you?"** *The blind man said to Him, "Rabbi,* **I want to receive sight.*** *Then Jesus said to him, "Go your way;* **your faith has made**

you well." And immediately he received
his sight and followed Jesus on the road
                              (Mark 10:51–52).

Bartimaeus was **convinced** Jesus could give
him back his sight, he had the **expectation** for
a miracle, and it was done to him **according
to his faith**.

When Jesus said to the father of the epileptic
boy, *"If you can **believe**, all things are possible
to him who **believes**,"* the father of the boy
tearfully cried out and said, *"Lord, I **believe**;
help my **unbelief!**"* (Mark 9:24). The young
lad's father was being exceedingly honest, he
had some faith, but he was acutely aware that
he was lacking the type of faith necessary for
the healing of his son.

        The disciples had attempted to cast out
the unclean spirit that had bound the boy
since childhood, but were unable to do it.
They came privately to Jesus and asked why
they could not cast the spirit out. So Jesus said
to them,

*Because of your **unbelief**; for assuredly, I
say to you, **if you have faith as a mustard
seed**, you will say to this mountain, 'Move
from here to there,' and it will move; and*

nothing will be impossible for you
                    (Matthew 17:20).

When the father of the epileptic boy asked for help, Jesus responded with, *"**O faithless and perverse generation**, how long shall I be with you? How long **shall I bear** with you?"* (Matthew 17:17). Would Jesus not say the same thing to our generation today? The Church of today is full to overflowing with unbelief.

After Jesus raised the twelve-year-old girl from the dead he passed on from there and *"two blind men followed Him, crying out and saying, 'Son of David, have mercy on us!'"* (Matthew 9:27). When He had come into the house, *the blind men came to Him.*

> *And Jesus said to them, "Do you **believe** that I am able to do this?" They said to Him, "**Yes, Lord**." Then He touched their eyes, saying, "**According to your faith let it be to you**"* (Matthew 9:28–29).

The latter statement from Jesus holds true for everyone who follows Him. You do not believe in miracles? *"**According to your faith let it be to you**."* You do not believe in divine healing? *"According to your faith let it be to you."* You do not believe that being clothed with power from on High? *"According to your faith let it be to you."* You do not believe in the devil? *"According to your faith let it be to you,"* and so with a hundred-and-one other things. It is all about believing, and *faith* is *believing*, faith is the *assurance*, the *expectation*, the *conviction* of things not seen becoming reality. Effectual *faith* can only come through absolute *conviction*—the *absolute conviction* that God can do anything. It is an other-world confidence that *with God nothing is impossible*. I have a perfectly whole, supernaturally repaired cup sitting in a china cabinet that conclusively proves that *nothing is impossible with God*.

Faith

The apostles said to Jesus, *"Increase our faith"* (Luke 17:5). So Jesus said,

*If you have faith as a mustard seed, **you can say** to this mulberry tree, "Be pulled up by the roots and be planted in the sea," and **it would obey you*** (Luke 17:6).

Faith is active, it is not a passive state. Faith requires regular testing and exercise in order for it to remain effective, and effective faith cannot increase until it is stretched to its absolute limit, and afterwards it requires regular stretching to its fullest limit:

> Therefore **take heed how you hear**. *For* **whoever has, to him more will be given;** *and whoever does not have,* **even what he seems to have will be taken from him**
>
> (Luke 8:18).

We must pay attention to **how** we hear: "*This is My beloved Son, in whom I am well pleased.* **Hear Him!**"

It was a Roman centurion who blessed the heart of Jesus because of his obvious faith. One day, when Jesus entered Capernaum, a Roman centurion appealed to Him on behalf of his servant, who was lying paralyzed at home. When Jesus made a move to go with the centurion, the soldier surprised Him:

> *The centurion answered and said, "Lord, I am not worthy that You should come under my roof. But* **only speak a word, and my servant will be healed.** *For* **I also am a man under authority,** *having soldiers under me. And* **I say to this one,**

'Go,' and he goes; and to another, 'Come,' and he comes; and to my servant, 'Do this,' and he does it."

*When Jesus heard it, He marveled, and said to those who followed, "Assuredly, I say to you, I have not found **such great faith**, not even in Israel!"* (Matthew 8:8–10).

The centurion's faith was an other-world faith. Although the soldier did not move in the supernatural realm in which Jesus and God moved, he perfectly understood the fundamental truth of authority. The centurion's *faith* in his rank gave him the *assurance* that following his orders he *expected* obedience, he had *the **conviction** of things not seen* being done. The soldier recognized Jesus' authority in the spiritual realm, and knew that Jesus only needed to speak and it would be done.

On another occasion Jesus and His disciples were going to a ruler's house, and they were surrounded by throngs of people:

*And suddenly, a woman who had a flow of blood for twelve years came from behind and **touched the fringe of His garment**. For **she said to herself, "If only I may touch His garment, I shall be made*** *well." But Jesus turned around, and when He saw her He said, "Be of good cheer, daughter; **your faith has made you well."** And the woman was made well from that hour* (Matthew 9:20–22).

Again, the woman had an **expectation** of being healed. She was **convinced** that if she could only touch Jesus she was **assured** of being made well.

One particular day Jesus went forth to the region of Tyre and Sidon (in modern-day Lebanon). And a woman of Canaan followed Him and cried out after Him saying, *"Have mercy on me, O Lord, Son of David! My daughter is severely demon-possessed."* Jesus ignored her pleas.

The disciples asked Jesus to send her away because she was a nuisance—continually crying out to Him. Jesus then told the disciples that He was only sent to the lost sheep of the house of Israel. However, the Canaanite woman came and knelt before Jesus, pleading with Him again, saying, **"Lord, help me"** (Matthew 15:25), but He answered and said, *"It is not good to take the children's bread and throw it to **the little dogs"** (Matthew 15:26).

The woman never flinched, and said, *"Yes, Lord, yet even **the little dogs eat the crumbs which fall from their masters' table"** (Matthew 15:27). Jesus responded by saying to her, *"O woman, **great is your faith! Let it be to you as you desire.**"* And her daughter was healed that same hour.

We see once again that a woman was totally *convinced* Jesus could heal her daughter. She had the necessary *expectation* that if she could only get His attention her daughter was *assured* of deliverance. Jesus virtually insulted her, calling the woman a "dog" because she was not of the house of Israel. Being called names never fazed the woman, she turned it around and said that even the dogs under the table received crumbs from their masters. Jesus relented because of the woman's great faith, and her daughter was immediately made well.

The above story shows the need to remain focused, to hang in and hang on despite setbacks. If we **believe, nothing is impossible—**

*But **without faith** it is **impossible** to please Him, for **he who comes to God*** *must believe that He is, and that He is a rewarder of those who **diligently** seek Him* (Hebrews 11:6).

Some days after Pentecost—the outpouring of the Holy Spirit—Peter and John were walking to the Temple at the prayer hour, near the area called Solomon's Porch, and they saw a beggar, lame from birth, looking to them for a charitable gift. Peter said *"Silver and gold I do not have, but what I do have I give to you."* He took hold of the beggar's arm and lifting him, said: *"**In the name of Jesus Christ** of Nazareth, stand up and walk!"* (Acts 3:6.). And the man's feet and ankles received strength and he jumped up and began walking and leaping in great joy. People came running together, and when they saw that it was the lame beggar who had always sat and begged outside the Gate Beautiful, they were filled with wonder and amazement.

So when Peter saw it, he responded to the people: "Men of Israel, why do you marvel at this? Or why look so intently at us, as though by our own power or godliness we had made this man walk? The God of Abraham, Isaac, and Jacob, the God of *our fathers, glorified His Servant Jesus, whom you delivered up and denied in the presence of Pilate, when he was determined to let Him go. But you denied the Holy One and the Just, and asked for a murderer to be granted to you, and killed the Prince of life, whom **God raised from the dead, of which we are witnesses**. And His name, **through faith in His name**, has made this man strong, whom you see and know. Yes, **the faith which comes through Him** has given him this perfect soundness in the presence of you all"*

(Acts 3:12, 15–16).

It was *faith* that gave life to the atrophied limbs of the beggar. It was Peter and John's *faith* combined with the lame beggar's *expectation* of *receiving* from them. The beggar had an *expectation* of *receiving*, but what he actually *received* was beyond his *expectations*. Often miracles go beyond all expectations, the unsolicited renewing of my cracked and disfigured cup is but one example. Miracles take place when there is *faith* and *belief* in *the name of Jesus*. When Jesus went to His own hometown in Nazareth to preach and heal He was scorned by the locals because they knew

Him and His family; thus its was written: "**He did not do many mighty works there because of their unbelief**" (Matthew 13:58).

Some Christians are often jealous of another person's particular gifting, some will even go as far as spreading malicious rumors about them. These people prevent miracles from taking place because of the air of **unbelief** that pervades the area and hangs like a pall over them. Jesus would have this to say to them:

> If I do not do the works of My Father, do not believe Me; but if I do, **though you do not believe Me, believe the works, that you may know and believe** that the Father is in Me, and I in Him
>
> (John 10:37–38).

Such people rob others of a possible supernatural touch from the Lord.

On a particular day after Jesus had crossed lake Kinneret by boat, He was met by a wild, naked man possessed by many demons. The demoniac was well known in the area and lived among the tombs and rocks and he would break the shackles and chains put on him to restrain him, and he cried out day and night and cut himself with rock. At first the demons resisted leaving the body they possessed, but Jesus finally allowed them to enter a large herd of pigs, causing them to run down the hillside and drown in the sea.

Losing a herd of some two thousand pigs caused great consternation among the villagers, they had been told about it by those who had witnessed the event. Everyone came out to see for themselves and they found the man,

> *from whom the demons had departed,* **sitting at the feet of Jesus, clothed and in his right mind.** *And they were afraid*
> (Luke 8:35).

Often, miracles take place and there is nothing to show that a miracle had taken place. However, the previously demonized man called Legion was found by those who knew him, sitting at the feet of Jesus, sane and properly clothed. No one could argue about that miracle having taken place. When Jesus got up to go with His disciples, the healed man begged to be allowed to go with Him, but He did not allow it. Jesus told the previously demon-possessed man to **"go and tell what** *great things God has done for you.* And he went his way and proclaimed throughout the whole area what great things Jesus had done for him" (Luke 8:39).

The people of that village believed that a miracle had taken place because the evidence was right there before their eyes—*sitting at the feet of Jesus, clothed and in his right mind.* The same with the man who was born blind whom Jesus gave sight to (John 9:1–38), not even the Pharisees and Priests could ignore it, before them stood the evidence. Nevertheless, they excommunicated the man upon whom Jesus had worked the miracle. In the china cupboard in our apartment sits the evidence of a miracle, many have taken the cup in their hands to look at it with absolute wonder.

Jesus said to Martha before He called Lazarus from the tomb:

> *Did I not say to you that if you would believe you would see the glory of God?*
> (John 11:40).

And would He not say the same thing to every churchgoer today? *Belief* in Jesus and *faith* in His name is all but missing from the Church of the 21st century. Want to be involved in God's work?—

This is the work of God, that you believe in Him whom He sent (John 6:29).

AS I have said elsewhere, Jesus, God, and salvation are no longer the flavor of the month today. God is being thrown out of nations left, right, and center. The name of Jesus is trashed continually and usually only mentioned as a swear word. Little has changed in this world in the minds of men in the past two thousand seven hundred years since the Prophet Isaiah penned the following about Jesus:

*He had no stately form or majesty that we should look at Him, and no beauty that we should **desire** Him. He was **despised** and **rejected** by men, a man of **suffering** and acquainted with **grief**, and as **one from whom men hide their face** he was **despised**, and we held him as **of no account*** (Isaiah 53:2–3).

So very little has changed, and the lack of appreciation for the **Prince of Peace**, the **author of our salvation**, lies with those who profess His name to those sitting in church pews, but who hide their faces and protect themselves from any form of persecution brought about by mentioning the name of Jesus in the hearing of those who despise His name.

In the Garden of Gethsemane, where, because of the agony awaiting Him, the sweat of Jesus *"fell to the ground like drops of blood"* (Luke 22:44), but His disciples then, as they do now, slumber on:

> *Then Jesus came to His disciples and said to them, "Are you still sleeping and resting? Look!, the hour is at hand, and* **the Son of Man is being betrayed into the hands of sinners***"* (Matthew 26:45).

Oh yes, slumbering church members have betrayed our Lord into the hands of an evil world. The number of adherents to Islam now outstrips the weak, materialistic, high-on-entertainment adherents of the Church. And the Church of Jesus Christ has had a six hundred-and-ten-year start on Islam. Shame! Shame on the Church!

Church Is Weak And Impotent

The weakest link in the Christian chain is that of materialism. A friend of mine, a pastor of an evangelical congregation in the U.S., told me that he owed $50,000 in Credit Card debt, and that it was choking the life out of him. He is not alone—many church leaders are swimming in Credit Card debt and it is drowning them, and not a few congregants have filed for bankruptcy because of debt. As I said earlier, Credit Card debt is the result of lust—lusting after what we cannot afford, and the Bible says this is *"covetousness, which is idolatry"* (Colossians 3:5).

In the parable of the Sower Jesus spoke about the seed, which is the word of God, falling among thorns (Matthew 13:7; Mark 4:7; Luke 8:7). Luke goes further with that parable and leaves no doubt as to what Jesus meant by it:

> *Now the ones that fell among thorns **are those who, when they have heard, go out and are choked with cares, riches, and pleasures of life**, and **bring no fruit** to maturity* (Luke 8:14).

Western Christianity is literally dying for lack of love and zeal for Jesus!

Jesus had some harsh words for all those who are playing "church":

*Strive to enter through the **narrow gate**, for **many**, I say to you, will seek to enter **and will not be able**. When once the Master of the house has risen up and shut the door, and you begin to stand outside and knock at the door, saying, "Lord, Lord, open for us," and He will answer and say to you, "I do not know you, where you are from," then you will begin to say, "We ate and drank in Your presence, and You taught in our streets." But He will say, "I tell you I do not know you, where you are from. Depart from Me, all you workers of iniquity." There will be weeping and gnashing of teeth, when you see Abraham and Isaac and Jacob and all the prophets in the kingdom of God, and yourselves thrust out. They will come from the east and the west, from the north and the south, and sit down in the kingdom of God* (Luke 13:24–29).

Again, Jesus said:

*Not everyone who says to Me, 'Lord, Lord,' shall enter the kingdom of heaven, **but he who does the will of My Father** in heaven* (Matthew 7:21).

Of Sheep And Goats

When the Son of Man comes in His glory, and all the holy angels with Him, then He will sit on the throne of His glory. All the nations will be gathered before Him, and He will separate them one from another, as a shepherd **divides his sheep from the goats**. And He will set **the sheep on His right hand**, but **the goats on the left**. Then the King will say to those on His right hand, "Come, you blessed of My Father, inherit the kingdom prepared for you from the foundation of the world: for I was hungry and you gave Me food; I was thirsty and you gave Me drink; I was a stranger and you took Me in; I was naked and you clothed Me; I was sick and you visited Me; I was in prison and you came to Me."

Then the righteous will answer Him, saying, "Lord, when did we see You hungry and feed You, or thirsty and give You drink? When did we see You a stranger and take You in, or naked and clothe You? Or when did we see You sick, or in prison, and come to You?" And **the King will answer and say to them, "Assuredly,**

I say to you, inasmuch as you did it to one of the least of these My brethren, you did it to Me."

Then He will also say to those on the left hand, "Depart from Me, you cursed, into the everlasting fire prepared for the devil and his angels: for I was hungry and you gave Me no food; I was thirsty and you gave Me no drink; I was a stranger and you did not take Me in, naked and you did not clothe Me, sick and in prison and you did not visit Me."

Then they also will answer Him, saying, "Lord, when did we see You hungry or thirsty or a stranger or naked or sick or in prison, and did not minister to You?" Then **He will answer them, saying, "Assuredly, I say to you, inasmuch as you did not do it to one of the least of these, you did not do it to Me."** And these will go away into everlasting punishment, but the righteous into eternal life (Matthew 25:31–46).

Feeding the hungry; visiting the widow and the orphan; visiting prisons and sharing the gospel with those incarcerated; providing for the world's poor; all these things are necessary practices to those called by the name of Jesus. The above New Testament teaching is reflected in God Almighty's own words:

*Is this not the fast that **I have chosen**:*
*To **loose** the bonds of wickedness,*
*To **undo** the heavy burdens,*
*To **let** the oppressed go free,*
*And that you **break** every yoke?*
*Is it not to **share** your bread with the*
  hungry,
*And that you **bring** to your house the*
  poor who are cast out;
*When you see the naked, that you **cover***
  him,
*And **not hide yourself** from your own*
  flesh?
Then your light shall break forth like the
  morning,
Your healing shall spring forth speedily,
And your righteousness shall go before
  you;
*The **glory of the Lord shall be your rear***
  guard (Isaiah 58:6–8).

Being a follower of Jesus is not *passive religion*, it is an *active occupation* with divine benefits.

Talents According To Ability

For the kingdom of heaven is like a man traveling to a far country, who called his own servants and delivered his goods to them And to one he gave five talents, to another two, and to another one, **to each according to his own ability**; *and immediately he went on a journey. Then he who had received the five talents went and traded with them, and made another five talents* (hundredfold increase). *And likewise he who had received two gained two more also* (hundredfold increase). *But he who had received one went and dug in the ground, and hid his lord's money* (no increase, he hid his talent). *After a long time the lord of those servants came and settled accounts with them.*

"So he who had received five talents came and brought five other talents, saying, 'Lord, you delivered to me five talents; look, I have gained five more talents besides them.' His lord said to him, "Well done, good and faithful servant; you were faithful over a few things, I will make you ruler over many things. Enter into the joy of your lord.' He also who had

received two talents came and said, "Lord, you delivered to me two talents; look, I have gained two more talents besides them.' His lord said to him, "Well done, good and faithful servant; you have been faithful over a few things, I will make you ruler over many things. Enter into the joy of your lord.'

"Then he who had received the one talent came and said, 'Lord, I knew you to be a hard man, reaping where you have not sown, and gathering where you have not scattered seed. And I was afraid, and went and hid your talent in the ground. Look, there you have what is yours.'

"But his lord answered and said to him, 'You wicked and lazy servant, you knew that I reap where I have not sown, and gather where I have not scattered seed. So you ought to have deposited my money with the bankers, and at my coming I would have received back my own with interest. So **take the talent from him, and give it to him who has ten talents**.

"For **to everyone who has, more will be given**, and he will have abundance; but **from him who does not have, even** *what he has will be taken away. And cast the unprofitable servant into the outer darkness.* There will be weeping and gnashing of teeth (Matthew 25:14–29).

Jesus said, "*The harvest truly is great, but the laborers are few*" (Luke 10:2). God never asks us to do more than we are physically able to do. Every member of the Body of Christ has been given talents *according to their own abilities*. Many members bring a hundredfold into the kingdom of God according to the talents given them. Sadly, most seem to hide their talents in their buttocks and sit on them, they are unfruitful and add nothing to the kingdom. Such people are in for an extremely rude awakening when the King returns to claim His own.

There are simply too many warnings for us to ignore. The New Testament has a plethora of extremely dire warnings for all who call themselves Christian. We are enjoined to **Hear!**, to **Listen**, and to **Understand**. Addressing one of the significant churches in the early days of Christianity, Jesus said:

I know your works, that you are neither cold nor hot. I could wish you were cold or *hot. So then, **because you are lukewarm**, and neither cold nor hot, I will vomit you out of My mouth* (Revelation 3:15–16).

We need to be ever mindful and not forget that *"Jesus Christ is the same yesterday, today, and forever"* (Hebrews 13:8). If Jesus was sickened by lukewarm Christians in the early years of Christianity, He will also be sickened by lukewarm Christians today and will spit them out.

The shortest verse in the Bible is John 11:35—"Jesus wept." The tears that he shed were not for His friend Lazarus who had died, but for the total unbelief that engulfed the people as he went to the site of Lazarus' tomb. Jesus had earlier said to Martha, the sister of Lazarus: *"Did I not say to you that **if you would believe** you would see the glory of God?"* (John 11:40), but Martha did not then grasp the portent of that moment.

Jesus came to the tomb where all people were weeping and wailing over Lazarus. Jesus wept because of the people's lack of **expectation** for the miraculous, the people's lack of **conviction** that **with God all things are possible**. Jesus told them to take away the stone from the entrance of the tomb and Martha displays her unbelief when she says, *"Lord, by this time **there is a stench**, for he has **been dead four days**"* (John 11:39). Jesus likely said to Himself: *"O faithless generation, how long shall I be with you? How long shall I bear with you?* (Mark 9:19) and then He cried out in a loud voice, *"Lazarus, come forth!"* And out came Lazarus wrapped in linen grave clothes, and if Jesus had not called Lazarus by name **all** the dead would have resurrected.

When we have a vital, intimate relationship with Jesus, we understand that it is no trouble for Him to raise the dead. I am fortunate, I have a very special cup on display in a china cabinet that was miraculously made new again after months of being badly cracked and chipped. I never asked for it to be made new, but am delighted that it was, and it was even restored without my knowledge of it having been done. That could only have been done by an all-powerful God whose depth of love is deeper than the deepest ocean.

The second recorded occasion that Jesus wept was over Jerusalem, *"the city of the great King"* (Psalms 48:2):

*As He drew near, He saw the city and wept over it, saying, "**If you had known**, even you, especially in this your day, the things that make for your peace! But now they are hidden from your eyes. For days will come upon you when your enemies will build an embankment around you, surround you and close you in on every side, and level you, and your children within you, to the ground; and they will not leave in you one stone upon another, **because you did not know the time of your visitation**"* (Luke 19:41–44).

They did not know **the time of their visitation** by God incarnate. The **did not believe** that Jesus was the Christ of God. They neither believed His words, nor believed His works. They were **unrepentant unbelievers** like many in today's 21st century Church.

In the second and third chapters of the book of Revelation Jesus addressed the seven great churches of Asia. It is notable that He addressed seven churches but *eight* times He calls for them to "*Repent*." Will He not call for all of Christendom's churches to also *repent* today?

Once again, addressing the early churches, Jesus said:

> *Behold,* **I stand at the door and knock. If anyone hears My voice and opens the door, I will come in to him and dine with him,** *and he with Me* (Revelation 3:20).

Jesus stands at the door of our hearts, knocking. In our lukewarm, anything-goes Church culture one only hears the above verse used in the context of Jesus knocking at hearts of the unsaved, but it is on the doors of **Christian hearts** that He is knocking. Is your "heart burning?" If you hear Jesus knocking at your heart's door as you read this, stop reading and open both the door and your heart wide to Him. Yesterday cannot be recalled, tomorrow cannot be assured, only today, this moment, is yours.

Faith Has The Last Word

Jesus is risen. If this was not a well-substantiated fact the gospel would be found to be untrue, as would also the divinely inspired apostles who would be indicted for peddling lies. But Jesus did rise from the dead and millions over two millennium testify that he changed their lives and gave them a divine hope, which the Apostle Peter expressed so well:

> *Blessed be the God and Father of our Lord Jesus Christ, who according to His abundant mercy* **has begotten us again to a living hope through the resurrection of Jesus Christ from the dead,** *to an inheritance incorruptible and undefiled and that does not fade away, reserved in heaven for you, who are* **kept by the power of God through faith** *for salvation ready to be revealed in the last time*
> (1Peter 1:3–5).

It is a *"living hope"* and a living *faith* that Peter speaks of. There is also **dead hope** and **dead faith** and, sadly, Jesus informs us more than once that many who think they have a *"living hope"* have in fact a **dead hope**, and their faith, if any, is misplaced.

> *The righteousness of God* **is revealed from faith to faith;** *as it is written, "***The just shall live by faith** (Romans 1:17).

> **The just shall live by faith;** *but* **if anyone draws back, My soul has no pleasure in him** (Hebrews 10:38).

Faith is total **belief** in an omnipotent God with whom **nothing is impossible—if you believe.**

It would be negligent of me not to challenge my readers with the same urgency and fervor that the Apostle Paul challenged the worldly Corinthian church:

> **Examine yourselves** as to whether you are in the faith. **Test yourselves. Do you not know yourselves,** that Jesus Christ is in you?**—unless indeed you are disqualified** (2Corinthians 13:5).

If you *failed* the *test:* **Repent!** If you passed the test: *look up!*

> *for now our salvation is **nearer** than when we first believed* (Romans 13:11).

The Church is *"the body of Christ"* (Colossians 1:24), and *"we are members of His body"* (Ephesians 5:30). The Church of today is lame, sick, and broken. If it returns to 1st-Century faith and belief *in* Jesus and His *power*, He will renew His beloved Church as easily as He renewed my beloved cup.

Ramon Bennett, the author of this book, also writes the *Update*, the regular newsletter of the *Arm of Salvation Ministries*. The *Update* keeps readers informed on world events that affect Israel, and also, on the ministry of Ramon Bennett and his wife, Zipporah. An annual donation of $20.00 is requested for the *Update*, which is available only by e-mail in digital PDF format. Subscriptions to the *Update* and any love gifts should be made via PayPal: <payments@shekinahbooks.com>.

Arm of Salvation (AOS) was founded by Ramon Bennett in 1980 and is an indigenous ministry dependent upon gifts and the proceeds from its book and music sales to sustain its work in and for Israel and the Jewish people. These are critical times for Israel so financial support is both needful and appreciated.

Copies of *My Cup Runneth Over* and other books by Ramon Bennett (see following pages) are available from *Amazon.com*.

Albums of popular Hebrew worship songs composed by Zipporah Bennett, are available by contacting Zipporah at the following e-mail address: <usa@shekinahbooks.com>.

Visit the website:
http://www.shekinahbooks.com
to subscribe, and/or donate via PayPal.

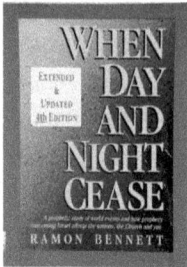

fourth edition

*"**WHEN DAY & NIGHT CEASE** is the most comprehensive, factual and informative book on Israel—past, present and future. If you want a true picture of how Israel is falling into Bible prophecy today, look no further. You will want to read this book"*

324 pages – Paperback, or Kindle e-book

PHILISTINE 2 lays bare the Arab mind, Islam, the Koran, the United Nations, the news media, rewritten history, and the Israeli-PLO peace accord. **PHILISTINE** will grip you. **PHILISTINE** will inform you. Philistine will shock you. Until you read **PHILISTINE** you will never understand the Middle East—the world's most volatile region.

364 pages – Paperback, or Kindle e-book

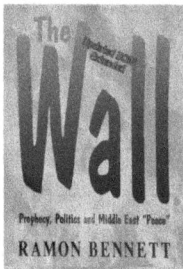

*"**They lead My people astray**, saying 'Peace!' when there is no peace"* (Ezekiel 13:10).

The Wall exposes the Israel-Arab peace process for what it is, an attempt to break Israel down "piece" by "piece." This book contains information the mainstream media, the CIA, the White House, and others would rather you did not know.

367 pages – Paperback, or Kindle e-book

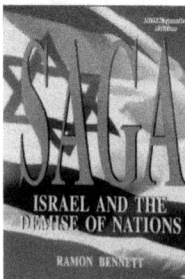

UNDERSTAND the chaos taking place around the world today! **SAGA** shows that Jews died because cruelty and evil and anti-Semitism are not confined to one race or nation but are found everywhere. **SAGA** is about Israel and Israel's God; about war and judgment—past, present, and future. Nations came and went, empires rose and fell; and God is still judging nations today. A "must read" in light of world events today.

284 pages – Paperback, or Kindle e-book

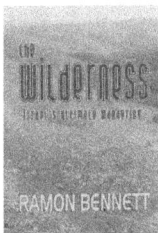

THE WILDERNESS: *"VERY INFORMATIVE BOOK FOR THOSE WHO* are looking for answers to what is happening in the middle east. God's Word is truth and Ramon Bennett breaks down verses that I've wondered about for years. A very good read, you won't be able to put it down." — William D. Douglas

335 pages – Paperback, or Kindle e-book

An accurate account of the events that led up to, and took place during, Israel's Operation Protective Edge, the 50-day war against Hamas in Gaza in 2014. It is a factual account of what took place, when it took place, why it took place, and the result of it having taken place. .

134 pages – Paperback, or Kindle e-book

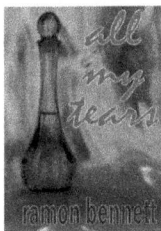

RAMON BENNETT has been introduced as "someone who has suffered the trials of Job."

Often verging on the unbelievable, *ALL MY TEARS* is Ramon's astounding autobiographical testimony; a story of an unwanted, abused child whom God adopted and anointed, and uses around the world for His glory.

448 pages – Paperback, or Kindle e-book

HISTORY, the gospels of Matthew, Mark, Luke, and John blended together in a ground-breaking uninterrupted read.

The **Color Print Edition** shows from where each interpolated piece comes from. Bible Students find this book fascinating. A Black Print Edition also available.

184 pages – Paperback, or Kindle e-book

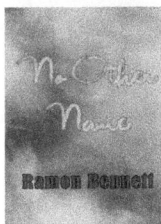

An edifying and informational feast for students of the Bible. Some of the more obscure sayings of Jesus are dealt with in Endnote expositions (mini Bible Studies) by the author throughout his ground-breaking continuous gospel narrative.

292 pages – Paperback, or Kindle e-book

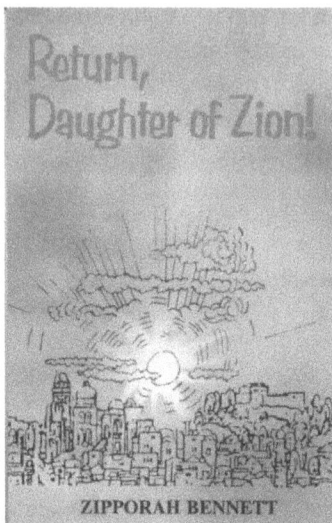

Return, Daughter of Zion!

Zipporah Bennett's testimony and autobiography. Read how Zipporah, a God-hungry Orthodox Jewish girl, found the Reality she longed for. This book, often amusing, will help the reader better understand the way Jewish people think and feel about the "Christian" Jesus.

137 pages – Paperback, or Kindle

Available on *Amazon.com*

Hebrew worship from one of Israel's foremost composers of Messianic worship songs

Hallelu

"Hallelu" –

Dual Hebrew–English songs of worship

Kuma Adonai

"Arise O Lord!"

Songs of warfare and worship

Mi Ha'amin?

"Who Hath Believed?"

Hebrew and Aramaic prophecies in song

For a descriptive overview or to purchase the above CD albums go to:

http://www.shekinahbooks.com

All books advertised in these are available from *Amazon.com*